CW00537651

True Love

What the Bible says
about relationships
and marriage

*Dr Chris Richards
and Dr Liz Jones*

EP BOOKS

Pistyll Hall, Pistyll, Holywell, UK, CH8 7SH

web: http://www.epbooks.org

e-mail: sales@epbooks.org

EP Books are distributed in the USA by:
JPL Distribution
3741 Linden Avenue Southeast
Grand Rapids, MI 49548
E-mail: orders@jpldistribution.com
Tel: 877.683.6935

British Library Cataloguing in Publication Data available

ISBN: 978-1-78397-023-0

It takes courage to write a book about God's standards on relationships and sex, and it will take courage to read it. But Chris Richards and Liz Jones have dared to be honest, spelling out the joys and responsibilities of living as God intended. To take this on board will save many tears and heartaches, bringing fulfilment and pleasure in their place. This is a book for everyone to read.

Roger Carswell, Evangelist

Young Christians today are confronted with many questions and choices about relationships. Dr Liz Jones and Dr Chris Richards look to God's Word for answers to these questions, showing that following God's pattern for living leads to real happiness. Whether we are single or married, we are set free to love God and serve others.

Dr Sharon James, author and conference speaker

CONTENTS

1

Introduction

As a young person living in the twenty-first century, following God's ways in the area of relationships is increasingly difficult. There is often a battle in our hearts between the attraction of the ways of the world and obedience to God (Galatians 5:17). Unless you are properly prepared for the battle, it is so easy to be drawn away by the world's loud voice. Here are just a few of the messages that you will be constantly exposed to:

- You're missing out if you don't have sex.

- Marriage is out of date.

- Casual sex is OK.

- Sex is the goal of a night out.

- Sex is all about me and my satisfaction.

- Sex can be experienced without consequences.

- There are no rights and wrongs in relationships, just what we prefer.

- Sex is a means of securing love.

All the messages above are lies or half-truths, but they are also powerful and tempting. As Christians, we need to be on our guard when we hear such messages because there is so much at stake. God has saved us through the work of Jesus on the cross in order that we may live a life of holiness through obedience. We are encouraged to strive for holiness: 'as he who called you is holy, so also be holy in all your conduct' (1 Peter 1:15). Holiness is not an add-on, but the very heart of our daily walk with our heavenly Father. The Bible repeatedly reminds us that our thoughts and actions in relationships affect other people and really matter to God, who commanded us to 'love your neighbour as yourself' (Matthew 22:39).

To be successful in this battle for holiness in relationships, you need to know exactly what you believe and why, so that you can respond wisely and swiftly to difficult situations as they arise. For this purpose God has given you His word, the Bible, where you can be sure to find clear directions on sexual purity: 'How can a young man keep his way pure? By guarding it according to your word' (Psalm 119:9). To help you understand His word, God gives you the Holy Spirit, who also motivates you and strengthens you to apply His word to your life. You are not alone in this struggle!

You are not alone in this struggle!

The Bible tells us that God blesses those who obey Him (Psalm 18:20). However, we are also warned that, because obedience is very important to God, the consequences of disobedience can be severe (Psalm 89:30–32). Though God offers us complete forgiveness (see Chapter 9), we may have to live with the earthly consequences of our sin for the rest of our lives. Nowhere is this clearer than in God's gift of sex.

Even when we are obedient, God does not necessarily give us all our desires. But as we pray for God's will to be done, He strengthens us and teaches us patience. Part of faith is trusting that His provision and timing are best.

We hope that this book will help you to know more about God's ways and desires for you in this area of your life. Our prayer is that it will help you to 'give careful thought to the paths for your feet and [to] be steadfast in all your ways' (Proverbs 4:26 NIV).

2

Singleness and marriage

Only two ways to live

We all start our lives as single people (and for the purposes of this book, by 'single' we mean unmarried). If you are reading this book, it is likely you are still single—though choosing to read a book entitled 'True Love' might suggest that you are wondering whether the situation will continue forever.

There are only two ways to live—single or married—and both states are gifts from God. The Bible makes it clear that singleness is a gift which all Christians have unless or until they receive the other gift of marriage (1 Corinthians 7:7). Recognising each as a gift means that, whether we are single or married, we can trust that God is sovereign over our situation, and will use our circumstances for our good and the good of others.

Pleasing God in our lives

- The two states of life that are pleasing to God are single and sexually inactive, or married and sexually active. *Matthew 19:3–12*

- Seek to honour God above everything. *Matthew 6:33*

Singleness—a gift from God [1]

Being single allows a Christian to serve the Lord in a way that is impossible for the married person. Paul writes, 'I want you to be free from anxieties. The unmarried man is anxious about the things of the Lord, how to please the Lord. But the married man is anxious about worldly things, how to please his wife, and his interests are divided. And the unmarried or betrothed woman is anxious about the things of the Lord, how to be holy in body and spirit. But the married woman is anxious about worldly things, how to please her husband.' (1 Corinthians 7:32–34).

Jesus tells us that some people remain single 'for the sake of the kingdom of heaven' (Matthew 19:12). For some people this may be for a period of time, but for others the single state may be life-long. A few people recognise that they have been set apart by the Lord for singleness for a specific purpose e.g. being a missionary in a particular situation where marriage would be difficult. But for many single people God seems only to reveal his plans one step at a time—and there is no certainty that they will remain single for a longer or shorter phase of their life. God may open up new circumstances and things can change very fast. Finding oneself single may be difficult at times but we must remember that those who give up anything 'for the sake of the kingdom' will be rewarded many times over, both in this life and in eternity (Matthew 19:29).

Being single allows you to live a life of undivided service to the Lord. In fact, the whole church is blessed when a single person serves God and the community in this way. Mark describes his experience as a single man:

> *Being single allows you to live a life of undivided service to the Lord.*

I have often experienced the well-intentioned pressure of family and friends, who assume, often without saying so, that singleness is abnormal and should be avoided at all costs. Yet, as someone who has led a chaste life, I know that I would not have been able to achieve the many things for God that I have, if I had been married with a family. The demands of work and family would have been irreconcilable.

I have experienced times of loneliness (though I know of some ill-matched and unsatisfactory marriages that are desperately lonely). However, I have learnt the importance of trusted and godly friends and with this provision my single life has been very fulfilling. No life outside God's will can fulfil. The important thing is to find contentment in the situation in life to which God has called us.

For a committed Christian, being single, with all its freedom, is not a gift to be given up lightly.

God has determined that the position you find yourself in at the moment needs to dictate your sexual state. If you are single, God requires you to be sexually inactive (sometimes termed 'chaste'). We know this from the discussion between Jesus and His disciples in Matthew 19, in which Jesus likens single people to 'eunuchs' who are compulsorily sexually inactive (Matthew 19:11–12).

Singleness ...

... is a gift from God. *1 Corinthians 7:7*

... allows you the freedom to work for the Lord without the concerns

and responsibilities of marriage.
1 Corinthians 7:32–35

Reasons for singleness

- Some people are single and sexually inactive through no choice of their own. *Matthew 19:12a*

- Some people choose to be single and sexually inactive for the kingdom of heaven. *Matthew 19:12b*

Marriage—a gift from God

Marriage is also a gift from God. God created marriage for loving companionship. He created Adam and observed, 'It is not good that the man should be alone' (Genesis 2:18). So He created Eve to be Adam's wife and this established the institution of marriage. The husband and wife must love, care for and support each other. God designed sexual intimacy to be a wonderful gift (Genesis 2:24) to strengthen this bond of love between a

> *God created marriage for loving companionship.*

husband and wife and as the means of having children.

Marriage has been designed to be the basis of each family unit. It is God's intention that children should benefit from being born and brought up in a family based on the security of marriage. We know from studies that children do best in a married family.[2] A child receives strength and security from knowing that their mother and father have promised to keep on loving each other, whatever the circumstances (Malachi 2:15).

❧

Marriage has been designed to be the basis of each family unit.

❧

Through childbirth, marriage is the means by which God has chosen to raise one generation after another to work and care for His world and so fulfil His command to 'be fruitful and multiply and fill the earth and subdue it' (Genesis 1:28). It is God's intention that all nations and their communities are made up of the building blocks of the family unit based on marriage.

The Bible makes it clear that sexual desire is to find its fulfilment in marriage and that, in general, those who are married are to be sexually active. In 1 Corinthians 7:5 Paul warns those who are married, 'Do not deprive each other of sexual relations, unless you both agree to refrain from sexual intimacy for a limited time so you can give yourselves more completely to prayer' (New Living Translation). One important reason for considering marriage is if you find yourself constantly struggling with unfulfilled sexual desires. Paul advised single people who could not exercise sexual self-control that 'they should marry, for it is better to marry than to burn with passion' (1 Corinthians 7:9).

Understanding marriage

It is natural to be interested in forming a romantic relationship with someone of the opposite sex. Love, sex and desire keep the pens of poets and song-writers flowing, dating and advertising agencies in business, and cinema goers anticipating the next 'chick flick'. Currently in our society such enterprises advertise, recommend and support a range of relationship types including one-night stands, short term relationships and living together. Amidst this clamour, enticement and pressure, it is a challenge to clear one's head and consider what a relationship between a man and a woman is all about—or, rather, *should* be all about.

For such a perspective we must turn to the Bible for that unique wisdom that only our Creator can impart to us. As knowledge of the nature, distance and demands of a marathon should affect the way a runner prepares for a race, so an understanding of the nature of marriage should influence all your romantic plans and sexual interests. For this reason, we are now going to look at some of the details of marriage given to us in the Bible.

> ❧
> *it is a challenge to clear one's head and consider what a relationship between a man and a woman is all about—or, rather, should be all about.*
> ❧

The design of marriage

Marriage was designed by God before the creation of the world. The first man and woman, Adam and Eve, were also the first husband and wife and this set a pattern for men and women to follow in the future for their blessing and benefit. Here are the words, at the start of Genesis, that first describe marriage:

'... a man leaves his father and mother and is united to his wife, and they become one flesh' (Genesis 2:24 NIV).

In these words, and others in the Bible, God has revealed the nature of marriage to us. His character is reflected in its design in at least three ways:

First, the design of marriage is *wise*. The nature of marriage should cause us to recognise the truth that the psalmist declares: 'How many are your works, Lord! In wisdom you made them all' (Psalm 104:24 NIV). God Himself has defined the character of marriage from the very beginning. Indeed, its highest spiritual purpose is to provide us with a picture of Christ's relationship with His church referred to in Ephesians 5:25. Man should, therefore, not try to redefine it as he sees fit.

We learn from Genesis 2:24 that God designed marriage as an exclusive relationship i.e. between only one man and one woman. This verse also highlights another important design feature of marriage—it brings together two people who are of a different sex. God has designed a man and a woman to be different—not only in their bodies, but also in how they feel and in the way they think. Because of these differences, men and women take on different roles in marriage. God designed Eve to be Adam's helper and companion (Genesis 2:18). It is God's intention that both the husband and the wife work together in a complementary way so that both they and their children benefit (to *complement* means to act together in different ways for the good of both). As the head of the family, the husband (Ephesians 5:23) should lead the family and take the final responsibility in providing for it, in

> *God has designed a man and a woman to be different—not only in their bodies, but also in how they feel and in the way they think.*

protecting it from threats (Ephesians 5:28–29) and in teaching his children (Ephesians 6:4). The wife is to submit to and support her husband in these responsibilities (Ephesians 5:22) and is likely to take special responsibility for running the home, and feeding and caring for the family. We see this illustrated clearly in the portrait of an 'excellent' wife in Proverbs 31:10–31, although in some circumstances, particularly with illness, the practical responsibilities may need to work out in a different way.

Secondly, the design of marriage is *good*. The character of all that God has created is 'very good' (Genesis 1:31). Marriage has been designed to be a blessing both to the married couple and to those around them. We may know of marriages damaged by unwise choices and sinful actions, but it is important to remember that the original design is excellent and can be trusted, when we act obediently and wisely. This is confirmed by God in many Bible verses, for example, 'He who finds a wife finds what is good and receives favour from the Lord' (Proverbs 18:22 NIV).

Thirdly, the design of marriage is *holy*. It is rightly described as 'holy matrimony'—not because the ceremony may be performed by a minister in a church building—but because it is a special relationship, different from all others, and designed by God. This is also true of sexual intimacy, which is a spiritual as well as a physical union. For this reason, when we talk about marriage and sex we need to do so carefully and respectfully. This also means that when we consider the prospect of marriage and intimacy ourselves, we need to remember that we tread on holy ground. We are accountable to God for anything we do to belittle or abuse marriage or sexual intimacy. It is also important that we respect the marriages of people with whom we have contact, for example at church, work or in other social situations.

> *'He who finds a wife finds what is good and receives favour from the Lord' (Proverbs 18:22 NIV).*

Marriage ...
> ... was created by God. *Genesis 2:24* and *Matthew 19:4–5*

> ... is a gift from God. *1 Corinthians 7:7*

God created marriage ...
> ... to provide companionship. *Genesis 2:18*

> ... to produce and nurture children. *Genesis 1:28*

The pattern of marriage

At the heart of getting married is the formation of a new family unit. When a man marries, he is to 'leave his father and mother'. At a wedding, the bride walks in with her father and then walks out with her new husband. This represents the husband and wife leaving their parents and joining together to form a new family as a married couple.

When a man and woman get married, they are 'united' in many important ways. The most obvious example of this is that they live together and share everything: decisions, food, money, surname and holidays. They also unite their bodies in sexual intimacy, which the Bible describes as the two becoming 'one flesh'.

The order in which this happens is very important. God's design for marriage is that a man and woman leave their family homes, are united in marriage and then unite their lives and their bodies in sexual union. Today, many people in our society choose to ignore this God-given order. Most commonly, they are sexually intimate with someone outside of, or before marriage. Others try to form a new family home before they have properly left their parents' home. Ignoring God's order in this way can lead to all kinds of problems.

> *many people in our society choose to ignore this God-given order*

The promises of marriage

The Bible describes the relationship of marriage as a 'covenant' (Malachi 2:14). This can be defined as a permanent commitment between two parties expressed in promises. These promises are made between a husband (bridegroom) and his wife (bride) on their wedding day. These promises, or 'vows', are made before God and those present at the wedding.

Here is one version of the marriage vows:

I, [name], take you, [name], to be my
    husband/wife;
to have and to hold from this day
    forward,
for better, for worse,
for richer, for poorer,
in sickness, and in health,
to love and to cherish,
till death us do part,
according to God's holy law;
and this is my solemn vow.

The words of the vows express the love that the bride and bridegroom have for each other. The word *cherish* is not often used nowadays. To cherish means to show your appreciation for someone of great value to you. A husband and wife cherish each other by looking after each other and wanting the best for each other.

This type of love could be described as

unconditional or *faithful.* Such faithfulness is expressed in three main ways.

First, it is expressed in their devotion to each other, whatever financial or health (or any other) circumstances develop during their marriage. This is clearly summarised in the words, 'For better, for worse, for richer, for poorer, in sickness, and in health'.

Secondly, God intends marriage to be life-long, only ending with the death of the husband or wife. They are to be faithful to each other through all the stages of life, right up to the infirmity of old age (if God permits longevity) and even to death itself, 'till death us do part'.

Thirdly, they promise to be faithful by 'forsaking all others'. That is, they commit themselves to an exclusive relationship. Sexual intimacy has been designed by God to strengthen the love between husband and wife. Therefore they should avoid anything that might tempt them to break the Seventh Commandment, 'Do not commit adultery'. Breaking this command might include pursuing sexual thoughts, words or actions towards or with anyone other than their husband or wife (Matthew 5:28).

Keeping the marriage vows is very important in maintaining the love of marriage. It is the security of the decision to love each other unconditionally which allows a couple to remain devoted to one another over the years. Dietrich Bonhoeffer described the truth clearly with these words, 'It is not your love that sustains the marriage, but from now on, the marriage that sustains your love.'[3]

Love in marriage

The idea of getting married often starts with romantic feelings. We can be sure that God expects married couples to feel romantic love for each other. The Song of Solomon is a stirring account of romantic love between a man and a woman anticipating, and then thrilled by, the joy of married union. The couple's love for one another is expressed in

'you have captivated my heart with one glance of your eyes' (Song of Solomon 4:9)

such comments as 'you have captivated my heart with one glance of your eyes' (Song of Solomon 4:9).

One husband, married for over a decade, wrote:

> Love is hard to describe but unmistakable when it is experienced. Love is a look, a smile, a connection, an emotion beyond words and without equal. Quite wonderfully and unexpectedly together with the person you love, in marriage you become one.

We should note that this kind of love is necessarily self-sacrificial. The Bible teaches that the husband is to love his wife 'as Christ loved the church and gave himself up for her' (Ephesians 5:25) and also to love his wife as his own body (Ephesians 5:28). The responsibilities of marriage are equally demanding for the wife. She is taught to 'submit' to her husband 'as to the Lord' (Ephesians 5:22). Both of these roles are a challenge. It is not easy to be a husband or wife as God intends.

How different is this love from the emotionally and sexually driven variety often promoted in the media, in which the main concern is of self-fulfilment rather than self-sacrifice, and the feelings of the moment rather than devotion of a lifetime! Such thinking has affected how people (even Christians) view marriage. Marriage has been redefined in terms of personal fulfilment rather than the promise of faithful and sacrificial love. With such high expectations of self-satisfaction, the most modest of difficulties or emotionally low times can be interpreted as a failure of a marriage, rather than an opportunity to express one's devotion to one another by patiently working at the relationship.

Marriage has been redefined in terms of personal fulfilment rather than the promise of faithful and sacrificial love.

Sometimes a husband and a wife need to *choose* to love each other—this is a decision not ultimately dependent on their feelings or what happens in their marriage. When two sinners live in close proximity and share their lives, time and possessions, the result is not always easy. There may be times when natural emotions and physical attraction are blunted by age and the demands of married life. The married couple must choose to rekindle the warmth of their emotions for each other by enjoying each other's friendship, putting the other person's interests before their own, by giving thanks to God for each other and by keeping the promises they made on their wedding day. In this way, a couple may expect their love for each other to deepen rather than lessen over the years. The Lord will also use this process to promote the growth of holiness in both husband and wife.

Sometimes a husband and a wife need to choose to love each other

The public nature of marriage

The vows of marriage are made in public. This is not simply because everyone likes to be involved in a good party! Rather, it is because an essential aspect of marriage is its public nature. Throughout the Bible, as well as in the present day, marriages are publicly acknowledged.

Marriage still has an important public as well as personal dimension. Society is changed and strengthened when a couple leave their existing family units and form a new and permanent one. Married families are the building blocks of society and provide it with stability. In contrast, a large number of chaotic and ever-changing relationships will give rise to a less stable society. You may sense that society is weakening all around; this is because marriage is being rejected by many and threatened by the increasing divorce rate.[4]

> ❧
> *Married families are the building blocks of society*
> ❧

The public nature of marriage allows both husband and wife to be held accountable for the promises they have made, makes others realise that the married couple are no longer 'available', and reminds their family and friends of their responsibility to keep supporting the couple in their marriage. Marriage is also a legal contract made before witnesses.

The design of marriage

- It is to be life-long. *Matthew 19:6b*

- It is to be between a man and a woman. *Matthew 19:4–5*

- It should be between only one husband and one wife. *1 Corinthians 7:2*

Additional points on marriage

- It illustrates God's love for His church. *Ephesians 5:25–32*

- It can provide protection from sexual temptation. *1 Corinthians 7:36*

- It is to be honoured by all. *Hebrews 13:4*

- It is demanding on time and energy. *1 Corinthians 7:32–35*

Marriage compared to 'living together'

It is now increasingly common for couples to 'live together' (cohabit) instead of, or before, getting married. It is often suggested that this could be helpful in finding out whether a couple are suited to each other, or whether or not they should get married. However, studies have shown that a couple who live together before they get married are actually more likely to split up than a couple who do not.[5] Thinking more deeply, perhaps this is not surprising as marriage involves the total commitment of a husband and wife to each other and is, therefore, not something you can just 'try out'. It is this commitment of marriage that gives a married couple the benefit of lifelong companionship and children the stability they need as they grow up.

> *a couple who live together before they get married are actually more likely to split up than a couple who do not*

Many studies highlight the benefits of marriage compared to living together:

- 58% of marriages last for life,[6] whereas most cohabiting relationships do not last long. The average duration of a cohabiting relationship in the UK is approximately 2 years before it leads to marriage or dissolves.[7]

- The instability of most cohabiting relationships has led to many single-parent families. Children born to a cohabiting couple have a 52% chance of seeing their parents split up by the age of 5 years compared to 8% for those who are born to married parents.[8] In addition, 93% of all 13–15 year olds who live with both parents, have married parents.[9]

- Couples who wait for marriage to have sex enjoy intimacy more.[10]

- Cohabitees are more likely to have an abortion, be unfaithful to their partner, get depressed, have alcohol problems and suffer domestic violence than married people.[11]

Going out

You may be thinking that you would like to get married some time in the future. But you may also be wondering just how you get to the point of deciding to marry someone, and what your attitude should be to sex until you decide to make your marriage vows. In our society, the most common way for a couple to proceed to marriage is by 'going out', so let us then look in some detail at what this is all about.

Just to get any language misunder-standings out of the way, by 'going out' we do not mean simply a one-off date, but a regular commitment to meet up with and get to know someone of the opposite sex. It actually means more than this, but read on!

What does the Bible say about going out?

Going out, as we know it in our society, is not really spoken about in the Bible. In contrast, the Bible emphasises the supreme importance of marriage in God's sight.

The limited Biblical references to going out may be because of the cultural differences between Biblical times and the present. Amongst the people of Israel there is evidence that many marriages were arranged by the bride and bridegroom's parents, as they are in many parts of the world today.

Though the Bible may not speak of going out as such, it does give at least one example of a friendship between a man and a woman that grew and led to marriage, that of Ruth and Boaz (Ruth

2:2–4:22). Notice how they 'check each other out'—not only regarding physical attraction (Ruth is aware of this as she follows Naomi's advice to wash and perfume herself, and put on her best clothes [Ruth 3:3]), but also regarding their characters (e.g. Ruth 2:20 and 3:11). As their friendship grows, so does the seriousness of their future commitment.

Thinking more about going out

We have noted the Biblical emphasis on marriage rather than going out. It is important, therefore, for us to consider further how going out relates to marriage. Going out with someone is more than a simple friendship. It has certain qualities which include:

- exclusivity (you do not go out with two people at the same time)

- public knowledge (some others will know about it)

- physical/sexual attraction

- commitment (at least for a time)

These qualities are shared with marriage and distinguish going out from simple friendship. Therefore, we would argue that going out should be considered as a time of getting to know each other, in order to test out if marriage is a future possibility. This being the case, it is not wise to go out with someone simply because you are feeling lonely or having a difficult time. If you could never imagine marrying them, then you should not be going out with them. Obviously, the certainty with which you can assess this will vary with how well you know him or her, and how carefully you have thought through exactly what marriage is. This is why people go out with each other for a while, rather than rushing into marriage.

> *going out should be considered as a time of getting to know each other, in order to test out if marriage is a future possibility*

Perhaps you are surprised at this perspective. Did you plan to go out with several people in succession without any serious assessment of whether marriage is a possibility? Surely, you think, this can do no harm. Here are some other things to consider:

- Going out requires a lot of time and energy. Could the time and energy used on a series of relationships be better spent in other ways (for example, by being involved in church life, developing hobbies, working hard or spending time with family and friends)?

- You may think of a relationship as short term, but does your boy/girlfriend think the same thing? Misunderstandings regarding where a relationship is going can cause much hurt. This is especially true if you decide to break up.

- Going out often makes people vulnerable to a new area of sexual temptation; this may not be a definite reason against going out, but a reason to take it seriously or to wait until you are closer to the age when marriage is a possibility.

- Most godly older Christians do not

look back and say, 'I wish that I had been out with more people' but 'I wish I had not been out with as many people'!

Do not make an idol of looking for someone to go out with

You may feel a lot of pressure to go out with someone. The more that your friends pair off, the harder it is to be the one who does not. If you are not going out with someone, you may receive all kinds of hints that you are missing out or are not normal.

> *You may feel a lot of pressure to go out with someone.*

It can be tempting to make looking for 'life's partner' the biggest priority in your life. However, we need to remember that our God is loving and sovereign, and has an intimate knowledge of us. He is working out all things for our good (Romans 8:28). It is so easy to be distracted from putting our energies into things of eternal importance. Jesus tells us to concentrate on God's kingdom and His righteousness, and all our needs will be met (Matthew 6:33). We can be confident in God's provision for us. A famous missionary to China, Hudson Taylor, found peace by placing this matter in God's hands:

> 'God always gives His very best to those who leave the choice with Him.'

What kind of person might you go out with?

Having learned about the nature of going out, you may be asking yourself the obvious question, 'What kind of person might I go out with?' Having explained that the purpose of going out is to test the suitability of possible future marriage, the question is really the same as, 'What kind of person might I consider marrying?'

Nothing has a greater influence on a relationship than whether there is a shared spiritual perspective.

Qualities to consider can helpfully be divided into three categories—spiritual, social and sexual.

Spiritual considerations

Nothing has a greater influence on a

relationship than whether there is a shared spiritual perspective. This is especially true for marriage, in which a husband and wife work together in every practical detail of life. Does your boy/girlfriend share your enthusiasm for God and His ways? Will you be able to encourage one another in your love for God's word, God's laws, God's people and most importantly, for Jesus as Saviour? Do you agree on the essential matters of your faith, such as how to understand the Bible and how to worship God? Is there the potential to help each other to grow spiritually?

Is it OK to go out with a non-Christian?

Christian young people often ask this question. The Bible warns, 'Do not be yoked together with unbelievers. For what do righteousness and wickedness have in common? Or what fellowship can light have with darkness? ... Or what does a believer have in common with an unbeliever?' (2 Corinthians 6:14–15 NIV)

The above passage reminds us that going out with a non-Christian represents the most extreme example of spiritual incompatibility. The word 'yoked' in the New Living Translation reads 'do not team up with', and this passage applies to all close partnerships between the Christian and non-Christian, which certainly include marriage and going out.

How can a believer and an unbeliever ever truly walk along the same path, sharing the same values, goals and understanding? If you decide to go out with a non-Christian, you will be ignoring God's Word and threatening your spiritual growth and peace.

Here is Karen's testimony. She can look back over her years of marriage with mixed feelings. The regret of her early disobedience, with its years of spiritual pain and uncertainty, combine with thanks to God for bringing her and her husband to the blessings of their present situation:

As a Christian I had told God that I would follow Him forever, but instead of handing over full control of my life and plans to God, I insisted that I had to have a husband and a family. I desperately wanted to be loved and to love someone. I met a lovely man and even though I knew that, as a non-believer, he did not belong to God's kingdom of light, I married him, thinking that I could soon win him over to Jesus. At the time I did not think we were so very different, as I was well aware that my heart, though in God's kingdom of light, had many dark parts to it. I felt that my new husband's heart, though still in darkness, had some light in it as he had some good qualities!

In the early years of our marriage I was generally happy, though at times I felt frustrated and lonely because he could not share with me my deepest desire ... for God. We had children and still he had not become a Christian. I feared he may die and not go to heaven. I worried that his lack of faith would damage our children's young faith in Jesus.

By God's grace, my husband became a Christian several years after we married. Since his conversion, I have felt relief from the single-handed responsibility of bringing up our children in God's love. It has also been very painful for us both to see that our relationship had lacked an honesty and depth that we can now have. I have grasped the massive difference between the hearts of believers and non-believers. When you have God's Spirit living in you, you are living in His light absolutely. Your heart is opposite to what it was.

Like Karen, you may think that by going out with someone you will eventually 'win them for Christ'. Karen had her hope fulfilled in this regard but she had no way to be sure. God makes no promise that your non-Christian boy/girlfriend, husband or wife will come to faith. Sadly, Karen's account is the exception. Usually the result is the other way round—the Christian leads a life that is spiritually isolated, frustrated by divided loyalties and a clash of life plans, and even pulled away from devotion to God. Let us look at Debbie's story:

> ❧
>
> *I have grasped the massive difference between the hearts of believers and non-believers.*
>
> ❧

When he asked me out I was a Christian, but I didn't go to church regularly. I started going out with him and he started coming to church with me but he didn't really believe. He did get baptised and confirmed in order to get married in a church, but once we had got married, his character changed, he became domineering and controlling and started to put me down. He didn't come to church and after a while stopped me going too. I lost my faith. After six and a half years, I left my husband and ended up in a women's aid refuge. It happened to be very near a church where I had some friends, so I started attending and later re-committed my life to God. I felt loved there and had a sense of belonging. I am now divorced and trying to bring up my son in a Christian home.

Social considerations

Friendship
Because marriage was created for companionship, it is important that the person you choose to marry should be your best friend.

We need to choose our friends carefully (Proverbs 12:26), especially the one with whom we will spend the rest of our life. A good friend will seek the best for you. It should also be a joy to care for them and look out for their best interests. A good friend will be trustworthy and will stick by you in hardship (Proverbs 18:24). Godly friends are the best of friends and should challenge

> ❧
> *A good friend will seek the best for you.*
> ❧

you when you make spiritually foolish decisions (Proverbs 27:17).

In deciding whom you should marry, it is important to consider whether you have some shared interests in addition to those that are clearly spiritual. It is also important to ask yourself whether you share perspectives on important practical issues such as money, work and lifestyle.

If you are single now, work hard to develop some deep friendships. These may act as an important preparation for the friendship of marriage, and will be a great blessing in themselves. You can learn more about the qualities of a deep friendship by reading the moving account of David and Jonathan in 1 Samuel 20.

Trust

Within a marriage there needs to be trust and open communication between a husband and wife. Therefore, you should have reservations about going out with someone if you cannot entirely trust that person.

Trust in a relationship is based on evidence and is built up as you get to know each other better. You will discover whether your boy/girlfriend always tells the truth, whether they always do what they say they are going to do, and whether or not they are truly open with you. You will see how they react and make choices in different situations, and you will discover whether you are able to trust their judgement.

You may also want to ask yourself whether they treat you with loyalty and respect, and whether it is easy to treat them with loyalty and respect.

Family

It is good to spend time together in the company of both your biological and church families. Both of these may provide wise observations (though not the final say, which is yours) about the suitability and quality of your relationship. Parents may have an important role here since they know more about you and your background than anyone else. Marriage is a family business! Going out is a time to consider how well you and your boy/girlfriend would get along with the family which you will be joined to if you marry. However, this should not compromise your future need and ability to form a new family unit when you do get married.

Remember also, should you marry, that it is likely you will have a family of your own. It is therefore important to ask whether you would be happy for that person to be the parent of your child, and whether you would be able to agree about how your children should be brought up. Men particularly need to consider whether there would be sufficient income to maintain a future home and family.

Sexual considerations

Appearance
In considering a relationship, appreciation

of physical appearance is important. The Bible recognises that there is such a thing as physical beauty e.g. Genesis 29:17 (Rachel) Esther 1:11 (Vashti) and 1 Samuel 16:12 (David). Men, especially, are initially attracted by appearance as well as by character. However, in our society which strongly emphasises the beautiful body, we

we need to be particularly careful of superficial assessments that only go skin deep.

need to be particularly careful of superficial assessments that only go skin deep.

A man may be attracted to a woman's figure, hair and face (all of which age) without considering her 'inner self, the unfading beauty of a gentle and quiet spirit' (1 Peter 3:4 NIV). A woman can be distracted by the thrill of attracting a man with her looks, but then is disappointed when he only has a shallow interest in her character and well-being.

Romantic desires
It is natural that you will experience strong emotions and romantic desires towards someone you are considering marrying.

Falling in love is a wonderful, God-given mystery and can help a couple to care for each other unselfishly.

Yet we have to be careful with these powerful emotions. In choosing whom to go out with or marry, it is easy to let your desires become dominant over the facts about your ability and suitability to proceed in the relationship. It is easy to 'fall in love' with someone who is unsuitable and very hard to realise this when emotions are running high.

It is easy to 'fall in love' with someone who is unsuitable and very hard to realise this when emotions are running high.

The decision to marry should never be taken on an emotional impulse. The depth and permanence of marriage demands that, as is said in the marriage ceremony, this way of life should not be undertaken 'carelessly, lightly or selfishly but reverently, responsibly and after serious thought'. Feeling deeply for someone is important, but the love which survives the demands of marriage has a much stronger commitment than that based on the first flush of feeling or the appreciation of outer beauty.

How to make wise decisions

- Be prayerful. *Matthew 26:41*

- Be loving and forgiving. *Colossians 3:12–14, 1 Corinthians 13*

- Be content in your situation. *Philippians 4:10–13*

- Take advice from the spiritually wise around you. *Proverbs 12:15* and *Proverbs 22:17*

- Avoid rash commitments. *Proverbs 20:25*

- Avoid ungodly peer pressure. *Exodus 23:2*

Going out in a way that honours God

Right ways to attract and appreciate

So much in our culture tells us that the only way to win attraction or show appreciation is through sexual provocation or arousal. This is unhelpful to a relationship and damaging to your spiritual life because it dishonours God. In contrast, the Bible teaches that, whether going out or not, young women need to cultivate an attitude of modesty (1 Timothy 2:9–10). This modesty is primarily directed towards men, and expressed through dress, actions and words. There is nothing wrong with displaying femininity attractively, but the challenge is to do this in a way that is not sexually provocative However, rather than focus her energies only on outward appearance, a young woman is to concentrate on seeking 'the unfading beauty of a gentle and quiet spirit, which is of great worth in God's sight' (I Peter 3:7 NIV).

There is nothing wrong with displaying femininity attractively, but the challenge is to do this in a way that is not sexually provocative.

For their part, young men need to radiate inner strength by striving for sexual purity. Testimonies indicate that it is more often men who push the physical boundaries whilst many women look back wishing that they had not gone as far as they did. They felt that it was expected of them and thought that it would please their boyfriend. In these circumstances the girlfriend should not feel shy about explaining this sense of pressure to her boyfriend. He needs to listen and respond lovingly by exercising self-control. Communication and thoughtfulness are vital in all stages of a relationship. Honour (1 Peter 3:7) is the moral attitude of a man which compels him to treat a woman with respect as the weaker sex, recognising her greater vulnerability to emotional manipulation by men (see Genesis 3:16) and, in most situations, her lesser physical strength.

Without compromising these attitudes, it is good to be able to show that you care about your boy/girlfriend by spending time together, listening to each other and helping each other. In all this, it is important to keep your actions in line with the depth and maturity of the relationship.

> *Do not expect your girl/boyfriend ... to be perfect. You will only be disappointed!*

Do not expect your girl/boyfriend (or in the future your spouse) to be perfect. You will only be disappointed! Rather, as you get to know each other better, remember to pray that the Lord would work in each of you to make you the people that He wants

you to be and the best that you can be for
His glory.

Emotional self-control

In addition to the physical self-control
which we have already mentioned, there is
a need for emotional self-control. It is
possible to let the powerful emotions of
being in love completely dominate your
thoughts. You need
to control them
rather than let them
control you. These
strong feelings can
easily lead to a
preoccupation with
each other that
excludes other
people. Such an attitude has damaged
many friendships or youth groups. You
may also find yourself without the support
of friends if your relationship breaks up.

*strong feelings can
easily lead to a
preoccupation with
each other that
excludes other people.*

If you are not careful, these powerful
emotions can also lead you to make rash
or unwise decisions. Peter warns us to 'be
sober-minded; be watchful. Your adversary
the devil prowls around like a roaring lion,
seeking someone to devour' (1 Peter 5:8).

If you go gently, you will be able to make sure that your (and the other person's) actions and responses come from a sincere and steady heart and discover whether there really is increasing affection for each other.

Going out means selflessness

We have already seen that the love of marriage is self-sacrificial. If going out is the time to see whether it is right for you to marry each other, it should also be a time marked by a self-sacrificial care for the other person, which reflects Christ's love for us:

'Therefore be imitators of God, as beloved children. And walk in love, as Christ loved us and gave himself up for us, a fragrant offering and sacrifice to God' (Ephesians 5:1–2).

A girl/boyfriend is neither to be treated as an object to show off, nor manipulated for our own selfish ends. In contrast he or she is to be appreciated, encouraged, supported and built up in his or her spiritual life. This is quite a responsibility and another reason not to take going out lightly. As one author has stated, 'There is far too much casualness, self-indulgence and unthinking selfishness masquerading as romantic love in relationships.'[12]

Setting the right pattern

Early on in a relationship, wrong patterns of decision-making and responsibility can be laid down and establish a bad pattern for married life. It is important to be sure, even at the stage of going out, that issues of leadership and submission are considered. This is an area where there is currently much confusion and pressure in our society.

The Bible makes it clear that there are God-given roles in a marriage (Ephesians 5:22–24). Husbands are designed to take the lead in the marriage relationship, and wives are to respect their husband's leadership and submit to it. It is important to note that a husband's leadership should be loving (Ephesians 5:25–30), modelled on Christ's sacrificial love for the church. This kind of leadership is firm, but gentle. It needs to be expressed by a willingness to listen. Wives are asked not to make this leadership difficult and allow their husbands to exercise the God-given role of ensuring the well-being of the family.[13]

Godly attitudes in going out and marriage

- Seek sexual purity. *Ephesians 5:3*

- Seek to obey God's word. *Psalm 119:9*

- Seek God's strength to be obedient. *Philippians 4:13*

- Be loving and forgiving. *Colossians 3:12–14, 1 Corinthians 13*

- Remember that obedience to God's commands brings fruitfulness and blessing. *Deuteronomy 30:15–16*

- Trust God's wisdom, not your own. *Proverbs 3:5–8*

- Trust God's good provision for His children. *Psalm 23*

Reasons not to marry

Going out does not always lead to marriage. After a period of going out, it may become obvious that marriage is not suitable and the best thing to do is to stop going out. It would be unwise to enter marriage half-heartedly or if you have serious reservations about your suitability.

It is right and proper to let your boy/girlfriend know and stop going out as soon as you are clear in your mind that you cannot proceed to marriage. Making this decision sooner rather than later will limit the

&

It would be unwise to enter marriage half-heartedly

&

hurt and disappointment that you may both feel. Sometimes people are tempted to get married for one of the following wrong reasons:

- they feel under pressure from their boy/girlfriend, family or friends. Only you can make the final decision and you must be sure that you really want to commit to the person in marriage.

- they feel sorry for the other person if they say 'no'. The decision to marry needs to be based on real affection and desire for commitment to the other person and not on pity.

- they think that there is nobody else who is suitable.

- they feel guilty that they have gone too far physically and think that they owe it to that person to get married. Making one mistake is no reason to make another. No one owes someone else a lifelong commitment. The response to sin needs to be to stop, repent and receive forgiveness.

Trusting God in disappointment

If you have been going out for some time and your relationship ends, you may feel very hurt and disappointed. Dashed hope may leave you spiritually and emotionally vulnerable. At such a time it is important to remind yourself that God is in control of a Christian's life and He promises that He will not leave nor forsake you (Deuteronomy 31:6). It may seem hard not to have your desires fulfilled but we must remember that God's ways are different from ours: 'For my thoughts are not your thoughts, neither are your ways my ways, declares the Lord.' (Isaiah 55:8). It is part of faith to trust that His provision and timing are best.

Keep close to God and He will strengthen you. Try to spend time benefiting from the comfort and companionship of family and friends. Avoid the temptation to immediately seek or rush into another relationship without being very sure of its suitability. It may also

It is part of faith to trust that His provision and timing are best.

be necessary to forgive the person whom you were going out with, or to acknowledge that you have done wrong in the relationship and ask them for forgiveness.

Proceeding to marriage

In contrast, you might go out with someone for some months or longer, at which point it becomes clear that you are well suited and that it would be right to get married. This is when a man might ask his girlfriend if she wants to marry him. It is also respectful and wise for the man to ask her father for permission to marry her, because up until marriage a father has the ultimate responsibility for his daughter's care. If his proposal meets with approval, then the couple become engaged.

Engagement is the time when a man and woman's plans to get married become public. It is not marriage itself and God does not intend us to be sexually intimate at this stage. It is important to realise that sometimes engagements end and do not lead to marriage.

Assuming your engagement proceeds to marriage, it is usually helpful during this time to attend some marriage preparation sessions with your minister or other older Christians in your church. You may gain from their wisdom as you anticipate facing the joys and responsibilities of married life.

Does the Bible really say that sex should be kept for marriage?

The circumstances in which we experience sexual intimacy are important to God. Sex is His design and He has determined with whom and when it should be experienced. 'In the beginning' God placed sex within marriage (Matthew 19:4–5) and that is where He means it to remain, so that the love of the husband and wife is strengthened and so that they may have children. The Bible is consistently clear from beginning to end that sexual activity of any sort outside marriage is wrong.

Having sex with a person who is married to somebody else is called adultery and is forbidden by God in the Old and New Testaments (Exodus 20:14 and Hebrews 13:4). If you are ever tempted to commit adultery, consider the severe and repeated warnings in Proverbs 5 to 7 about its social, financial and spiritual consequences. 'A man who commits adultery has no sense; whoever does so destroys himself' (Proverbs 6:32).

> ❧
>
> *'A man who commits adultery has no sense; whoever does so destroys himself'* (*Proverbs 6:32*).
>
> ❧

There are many references to sex in the New Testament. As we have mentioned, Jesus outlines two (and only two) states that please God—either married and sexually active, or single and sexually inactive (Matthew 19:3–12). In this account, Jesus is cross-examined about the possibility of divorce. The disciples are shocked at His uncompromising reply, which maintains the permanence of marriage and the sin of adultery. They respond by exclaiming, 'If such is the case of a man with his wife, it is better not to marry' (verse 10), thinking perhaps that a looser non-marital sexual arrangement is the alternative to the demanding exclusivity of marriage. But they are in for another shock because the only alternative that Jesus gives to the state of marriage is that of a 'eunuch', someone who is compulsorily sexually inactive, either because he has no choice or because he has chosen to be so 'for the sake of the kingdom of heaven' (verse 12). Jesus gives no hint here of permitting any sexual activity outside of marriage.

Further instruction to keep sex for marriage comes from the forbidding of 'sexual immorality' (e.g. 1 Corinthians 6:18, Ephesians 5:3). The word translated as *immorality* in many modern versions means any sexual activity outside marriage, including pre-marital sexual intimacy, adultery and homosexual acts.[14]

To seek sexual arousal outside marriage is to go in exactly the opposite direction to this command. God's word warns us to 'keep away from the cliff!' but by seeking sexual arousal, we selfishly go as close to the edge of the cliff as possible. Such an approach reflects a wrong attitude of heart, wanting to see how much we can get away with, rather than obeying God wholeheartedly.

Sexual purity begins in the desires of our heart. Jesus said, 'But I say to you that everyone who looks at a woman with lustful intent has already committed adultery with her in his heart' (Matthew 5:28). Jesus warns us against feeding our inner sexual appetite through thoughts as a substitute for the act of sex. (How difficult it is to avoid these thoughts in a society where so many sexually provocative images are used everywhere you look.) If what Jesus says applies to our thoughts, it must also apply to our actions. (See Chapter 6 for practical advice on how to respond when faced with temptation.)

❧

Sexual purity begins in the desires of our heart.

❧

Sex ...

... was created by God. *Genesis 2:24*

... is a good gift from God. *Genesis 1:31*

The purposes of sex ...

... to strengthen marriage. *Genesis 2:24*

... to produce children. *Genesis 4:1*

Sexual intimacy is only for marriage

- *Genesis 2:24*

- *Ephesians 5:3*

- *Hebrews 13:4*

- *Exodus 20:14*

Common reasons given for not keeping sex for marriage

'We're planning to get married anyway'

Being obedient to God means doing the right things in the right order. We have already noted the order in the Genesis account of marriage. Sexual union comes after, not before, union in marriage. A sign of true love is the willingness to keep to this order and wait. In such a way you honour God, your future spouse and yourself. You will also build up the ability to trust each other in the future. Remember also that engagement is not marriage and sometimes engagements do not last.

The run up to marriage is not only a much-needed time of preparation but can also be a time of testing to see whether it is wise to go forward to marriage. Going against what the Bible says and having sex with a person before marriage, can affect your ability to get to know them and assess their character. This was the experience of Emily, who says:

Sex led me into marrying the wrong guy. Being sexually intimate with someone confuses your true feelings. You imagine yourself to be in love when really it's just lust. You don't really love that person. If you weren't so intimately involved with them you would look at them entirely differently. I did think that I knew him very well because we were intimately involved with one another, but you don't know anyone just because you have sex with them. It doesn't mean you know that person in other ways, you just know them in a sexual way and all the rest is hidden.

'Marriage is only a piece of paper'

The marriage ceremony is not simply a man-made formality. God created marriage to bring a husband and wife together, 'What therefore God has joined together, let not man separate' (Matthew 19:6). The vows are made to each other in public and, most importantly, before God. As previously explained, the public nature of marriage makes it completely different from living together (cohabitation). This is still recognised by many in public life, as represented by the following comment quoted in a newspaper article:

> *the public nature of marriage makes it completely different from living together*

'There is something different about being married. People are bound together when they are married in a way that they are not if they are just living together.'[15]

'We need to try out the physical side before marriage'

Many people fear that not having a physical relationship before marriage will make them clumsy and inexperienced on their wedding night. However, it is actually the closeness of discovering something new together that brings much of the joy to early married sexual experience. Here is what a recently married couple said about this:

> Since being married it has become clear to us how important it is that sex should only take place within marriage. Because we waited until marriage, there is no pressure to 'perform' as neither of us have any past sexual experiences. This gives us much greater freedom to enjoy each other without the baggage of past memories.

Some are tempted to carry out a sexual 'test drive' before marriage. Sex outside marriage is so starkly different from sex within the total commitment of marriage that you would not be testing what you were trying to test anyway!

Temptation to be sexually intimate in a serious relationship is one reason

that the Bible gives for getting married
(1 Corinthians 7:36). Marriage is a
protection (although not a complete one)
from sexual temptation. You may think
marriage is not an option, for example,
because of competing interests such as
progress in your career. However, if you
are struggling sexually and wish to be
committed to each other, then consider
whether marriage is really impossible or
just inconvenient.

The Bible makes it quite clear that, as
one writer put it, 'if you are not ready for
marriage to one another, then you are not
ready for *sex* with one another'.[16] If you
have decided that marriage is not going to
be a possibility, you both need to step back
from the relationship, either in intensity
or completely, depending how radical you
have to be to avoid falling into sin.

We have just outlined three examples
of the kind of excuses and justifications
that people give for not keeping sex for
marriage. It is important to recognise and
reject worldly arguments (1 Corinthians
2:13–14), even if they sometimes seem
plausible. Be confident that the God who

made you knows what is best for you. 'Trust in the LORD with all your heart, and do not lean on your own understanding. In all your ways acknowledge him, and he will make straight your paths' (Proverbs 3:5–6).

If sex is for marriage, how physical should we be when we go out?

Sexual interest in the opposite sex is normal, not wrong—that is the way that God made us. Neither is sexual arousal wrong in itself—it sometimes just happens without us seeking or anticipating it. However, outside marriage we should certainly not seek out, nor give ourselves the freedom to enjoy, sexual arousal. This not only honours God, but also protects any future marriage from the intrusion of past sexual experiences with others.

What tempts one person will be different from what tempts another person and may be different for you and your boy/girlfriend. For some, kissing is too provocative. For others, even simply holding hands may encourage unhelpful or sinful thoughts. You need to ask yourself regularly whether what you are thinking, doing, provoking or seeking is consistent with an inner desire for a pure life that honours God. Jesus tells us to root out anything that causes us to sin (Matthew 5:29).

Once on the road of sexual arousal, it is a steep and slippery downhill path! Once sexually aroused, it is natural to desire more intimacy leading to further arousal and so on. This spiral of activity and desire is meant for a purpose! It is designed to prepare the body for full sexual intercourse in the right context of marriage. If you are going out with someone and find yourself regularly on this path, you will not only be placing a strain on your relationship but will be doing something wrong before God. One day you may not find a way of stopping the slide into full intercourse with its lasting consequences and profound regrets.

❧

practising self-control in your relationship will help to build up trust between you.

❧

In contrast, practising self-control in your relationship will help to build up trust between you. Such self-discipline may have lasting benefits, because if you do end up marrying your boy/girlfriend, it will make you feel more secure in your marriage. Young men are especially likely to be tempted to push the boundaries so that their girlfriend is always having to say 'no'. If this is the case and they get married, she may find it difficult to change her 'role' and relax in a truly fulfilling sexual relationship.

Practical advice

Consider the circumstances in which you may be tempted. Perhaps these are times when you are less accountable such as being alone in the house together, or when keeping your self-control is less easy due to alcohol or tiredness. There are practical steps you can take to avoid falling into temptation, such as avoiding provocative clothing, or spending time in a group setting rather than spending most of your time alone together. When you do spend time alone together, it may be helpful, for example, to leave the door open and avoid lying down together.

It is important to discuss between

yourselves what is helpful to avoid and to set boundaries for the physical side of your relationship (better in an unheated moment or it may make temptation worse). It may also be a good idea to tell a trusted friend the boundaries you have decided, and ask them to keep you accountable.

Young men should remember that a woman's desire for emotional security may lead her to agree to a level of physical intimacy that is not right before marriage. Young women should remember that being unthinkingly provocative in appearance and behaviour can lead a boyfriend into sin.

6

Facing temptation

Temptation is an enticement to disobey God by thinking, pursuing or doing something that is wrong. You may begin to think that obeying God is not the best for you or perhaps just less fun. Sexual temptation may take several forms. We have just looked at temptation whilst going out and later in this chapter we look at other areas of temptation linked to sexual purity.

We all need to be on constant guard against the attacks of Satan and to keep away from situations in which we know we might give way to temptation. Men are more often tempted by visual things and to sex outside of commitment, while women are vulnerable to wrong relationships by the attraction of emotional security and appreciation. Knowing that we face such things, our heavenly Father provides us with spiritual armour for our protection (Ephesians 6:10–18), so that evil need not take control of us (Psalm 119:133).

> ✒
>
> *Men are more often tempted by visual things and to sex outside of commitment, ... women are vulnerable to wrong relationships by the attraction of emotional security and appreciation.*
>
> ✒

How should you respond to temptation?

1 *Pray urgently* to the Lord for strength and protection (Ephesians 6:18 and 2 Thessalonians 3:1–3). Acknowledge the particular temptation before God and be ready to cry out as Jesus did,

'not my will, but yours, be done' (Luke 22:42).

2 *Remind yourself what the Bible says.* Satan not only provokes us to want wrong things, but also blinds us so that we do not realise that they are wrong. Satan succeeded in tempting Eve by casting doubt on God's word: 'Did God actually say ...?' (Genesis 3:1). You need to remind yourself of God's direction by reading the Bible (Psalm 119:9). Jesus repeatedly quoted Scripture to protect Himself against attacks of Satan (Luke 4:1–13). You may also need the counsel of a godly friend to help you recognise what is right and wise.

❧

Satan not only provokes us to want wrong things, but also blinds us so that we do not realise that they are wrong.

❧

3 *Avoid tempting places and circumstances* and firmly walk away from a compromising situation (1 Corinthians 6:18 and Matthew 5:29–30).

4 *Ask for the help of the Holy Spirit* and make a wholehearted decision to say 'no' to sinful desires. Ask for God's help and protection, particularly in any area where you are vulnerable (2 Timothy 2:22).

5 *Be encouraged* that in the discipline of resisting temptation God is teaching you to grow in your understanding of His will and is preparing you for heaven (Romans 12:2 and James 1:12).

6 *Share your situation* with a trustworthy Christian friend or leader in your church—ask them for prayer and be ready to answer for what you do.

Joseph avoided falling into sin by recognising that the temptation he faced would have led him to sin against God and by his overwhelming desire not to grieve God. He, therefore, took evasive action and ran away (Genesis 39:7–12). Remember, 'resist the devil, and he will flee from you' (James 4:7).

> *'resist the devil, and he will flee from you'* *(James 4:7).*

Specific issues

Pornography

The internet has made it easy to look at pornography without anyone else knowing. Many films and popular magazines also contain provocative visual material. Christians are not immune to temptations from these sources. Here are several reasons why using pornography is wrong and highly damaging:

pornography crudely cuts up a person, separating the object of our lust ... from the reality of the person

- Jesus warns us that lusting after someone in our minds and hearts is sinful (Matthew 5:28). As with other sins, it deadens our walk with the Lord and dries up the fruitfulness of our lives.

- By its nature, pornography crudely cuts up a person, separating the object of our lust (not just in the image but in our minds) from the reality of the person—their lives, thoughts, needs,

situation and how we relate to them.
Once our mind becomes used to this,
it can affect all kinds of relationships
that we have.

• This is all done for our selfish
  entertainment. The use of
  pornography is highly self-absorbing
  and self-centred.

• Pornography can be addictive.
  There is a hunger for more and
  more provocative images to produce
  the same stimulation. In addition,
  when indecency in print or in film
  fails to provoke, the person who uses
  pornography may turn to people with
  the frightening desire to de-humanise
  them for their own selfish ends. This
  process has been associated with
  many horrific crimes, including the
  actions of several serial murderers.[17]

• Pornography degrades and abuses
  those involved in making it and fuels
  prostitution and trafficking.

So beware of pornography. If you are
tempted in this area, take radical action

(Matthew 5:29–30). Make yourself accountable to a church leader or trustworthy friend who can, if necessary, challenge you as well as provide encouragement and prayer support. Change the environment of your home so that others are always around when you are on the internet (be careful about computers in unsupervised bedrooms). Make sure there is a high-level filter on all your internet access. Most importantly, ask God to forgive you for past sins in this area and for His strength to be obedient in the future.

Masturbation

The Bible does not directly refer to masturbation. However, we have already explained why you should avoid seeking sexual arousal with someone you are going out with. The reasons for guarding against this also apply to self-arousal.

Also consider:

- Masturbation separates a sexual act from a relationship, whereas sexual activity is designed to take place only within the relationship of marriage.

- We should not ignore our conscience's witness. Many testify to a sense of unease and guilt about masturbating.

- Although often used to relieve sexual tension, it can arouse sexual interest and fantasies, which may tempt one to increase sexual activity outside marriage.

Most people do not talk about masturbation because it is embarrassing, so you may not realise that many Christians struggle with temptation in this area. If this is a problem for you, God promises His strength and help: 'I can do all things through Him who strengthens me' (Philippians 4:13).

Homosexuality

Some young people have a sexual interest in those of the same sex. This can be a passing interest as the person grows up. However, for some such an interest remains or develops. The Bible makes it quite clear that giving in to such sexual interest by pursuing homosexual thoughts and actions is wrong, and has physical and spiritual consequences (1 Corinthians

6:9–11). Biologically and physically, it goes against the way God created people to be.

If you are troubled by homosexual thoughts, it is sometimes easier to accept the world's view that homosexuality is natural, and that there is nothing wrong with it, but this is clearly against God's teaching in the Bible. Rather than taking what may seem the easier way out, turn to a church leader or trustworthy friend who can provide prayer support, encouragement and accountability. You could also contact a Christian organisation which supports people struggling with homosexual temptation.[18]

Social networking

The Bible teaches that God made us to have a relationship with Him and to mirror that relationship here on earth, especially in marriage, and also with wider family and good friends. While there are benefits from using social networks, there are also many dangers and temptations which a Christian should carefully consider.

Although social networks facilitate

relationships with many people, it is worth considering the nature of these relationships and the motives behind them. It is easy for the focus of these relationships to be on yourself, rather than on the other person because you crave the attention of others and so present an unreal image of yourself. This is essentially idolatrous, where the idol is yourself. Social networks also allow people to connect without necessarily taking responsibility in the relationship. This can lead to bullying, provocation to be sexually explicit, adultery and even, in some cases, dangerous or abusive relationships.

> ❧
> *We do not have to spend time convincing the world and ultimately ourselves that we are worth something, because to God we are invaluable*
> ❧

Social networking can also soak up time so that prayer, Bible reading, serving others, and even our studies and work can be adversely affected. Remember that the Christian's identity is rooted in God and in His great love for us. Our purpose is to love and honour Him in our lives. We do not have to spend time convincing the world and ultimately ourselves that we are worth something, because to God we are invaluable (Matthew 6:26 and Jeremiah 31:3).

7

What might happen if you don't keep sex for marriage?

God's command to keep sex for marriage is full of His wisdom. Your obedience will not only glorify God but will also protect you from all kinds of threats—to your emotions, your body, your relationships, and the closeness of your walk with God. The Bible reminds us that 'the sexually immoral person sins against his own body' (1 Corinthians 6:18).

You will hurt

The expression 'one flesh' is very descriptive—it means that through sex we can and should become so close to our husband or wife (emotionally, physically and spiritually) that nothing on earth can separate us. God designed sex to strengthen marriage. It was never intended that someone would have sex and then walk away from the relationship. It therefore hurts and damages those involved if a sexual relationship ends. This can give rise to a wide range of painful emotions in ourselves and towards others—for example, regret, guilt, anger, sadness, depression and loss of self-confidence. Here is the testimony of Jane who looks back at her first relationship:

It was never intended that someone would have sex and then walk away from the relationship.

As a fourteen-year-old girl going out with an older boy, I felt that having sex was what was expected. It was not a great relationship and ended in two months. I am now twenty-eight and still feel the pain and regret of having given away something so special to someone who was not in a position to treasure it. Looking back, he has shared something of me that I should never have chosen to give him.

Because we give *ourselves* away in sexual union, it is our very heart, our value and identity, which is threatened so much if sex is abused. Sex involves utter vulnerability to another person. Without the security of absolute commitment, we are wide open to painful rejection and loss of trust. This can have dramatic effects on our state of mind and confidence as well as future relationships, as Ivan experienced:

I first had sex with my girlfriend when we were fifteen. I'd been going out with her for almost a year, and loved her very much. She was friendly, outgoing, charismatic. We'd done everything but have sex, and then one night she asked if we could go all the way.

A few days later, we broke up. It was the most painful time in my life. I had opened myself up to her more than I had to anybody, even my parents. I was depressed, moody, nervous. My friends dropped me because I was so unsociable. I felt a failure. I dropped out of sports. I started to fail at school. I didn't go out with anyone for ages. I was afraid of falling in love.

The outcome of Ivan's relationship is not uncommon. Teenage relationships outside marriage frequently break up soon after sex has taken place. Often it is the young man who walks away and there can be various reasons for this. He may have had his thrill

> *Teenage relationships outside marriage frequently break up soon after sex has taken place.*

and now wants to move on to the next challenge, or he may take fright at the greater level of commitment that the woman often demands once she has given herself fully to him physically.

Physical surrender without the complete and loving life-long commitment of marriage is inconsistent and sooner or later will break you up spiritually and emotionally. We, as paediatricians, see the effects of this in the young people we care for in our clinics and schools. Such damage can produce a range of physical symptoms such as headaches and tummy aches as well as effects of low self-esteem such as self-harm and eating disorders. If people experience the pain of the sexual bond repeatedly forming and breaking, they may try to protect themselves from the pain by (often subconsciously) trying to toughen themselves up emotionally. Like a wound, we will hurt and may later harden like a scar. But there is hope. There is one route to genuine healing of these wounds—through the forgiveness and love of the Lord Jesus. Only He can heal our pain and soften our hardness.

And sometimes the Lord graciously uses our sins in this area to draw us to Himself. Here is Tom's testimony:

I remain saddened by and ashamed of my past sexual experiences. But it was these that led me to long for a pure life and eventually brought me to my knees to ask for and receive forgiveness from the Lord Jesus. It is amazing to think that He was willing to use the depths of my sin to save me! Perhaps no other sin would have shaken me to repent.

You may get (her) pregnant

The oneness of sex is expressed when the sperm and egg unite to form new life. In the era of contraception, it is easy to forget that God designed sex to produce babies, and marriages to be fruitful. None of the commonly-used contraceptives can guarantee to prevent this happening.

> *In the era of contraception, it is easy to forget that God designed sex to produce babies, and marriages to be fruitful.*

Fourteen per cent of couples who 'typically'[19] use the condom conceive unintentionally in the first year of their relationship.[20] Unplanned encounters have much higher rates of pregnancy. And you do not have to have full sexual intercourse to get pregnant. Furthermore, deliberately ending the new life through abortion (or sometimes when the morning after pill is used), as many women are advised to do, breaks God's Sixth Commandment (Exodus 20:13).

It may be stating the obvious to describe bringing up a child as a demanding and long-term responsibility. It is God's design that a baby should grow up with the security of a family. Both parents have a God-given responsibility to bring up their children. This is another important reason for keeping sex for marriage.

You may get a sexually transmitted infection (STI)

Another consequence of sex outside marriage is catching a sexually transmitted infection (STI). The rising number of sexual partners has led to a rapid spread of these infections around the world, especially amongst young people. Rates of infection for the most common STI, Chlamydia, have doubled in the last nine years.[21]

It is God's design that a baby should grow up with the security of a family.

Sexually Transmitted Infections (STIs)— Did you know?

- The most common STI worldwide is Chlamydia.[22] This and Gonorrhoea sometimes cause a whitish mucous discharge from the genitals.

- Many people with an STI do not know they have one.[23]

- Sometimes Chlamydia and Gonorrhoea infections go unnoticed, but can cause infertility in women by blocking the fallopian tubes.[24] This may only become apparent several years after the infection.

- Several STIs, including Herpes and Human Papilloma Virus (HPV), are not curable with medicines and may be life-long.

- Women are more vulnerable to catching STIs than men. One reason is because the vagina is more susceptible to infection than a man's penis.[25] Women also suffer more health complications after sexually transmitted infections than men do.[26]

- Female teenagers are at highest risk of catching an STI.

- Many STIs can be transmitted by oral sex.[27]

- Those with one STI are more susceptible to another, especially HIV.[28]

The spread of STIs has not been contained by easier access to condoms and more teaching about their use. The increasing availability has actually increased spread of STIs by encouraging sexual activity outside marriage because people think (wrongly) that they can have 'safe(r) sex'.

Condoms and the myth of safe sex

- Condoms reduce the risk of infection, but they do not protect from any STI 100% of the time.[29]

- There is little evidence of reduced spread of the warts virus even with 100% condom use, though there may be limited protection from some consequences of infection including genital warts in men and cervical cancer in women.[30]

- Teenagers are less likely to use a condom after alcohol or drug use.[31]

Remember that the only way to be sure of a marriage without STIs is for the husband and wife to marry without having experienced any previous sexual intimacy and to remain faithful within marriage.

You will threaten your spiritual life

Though the physical consequences of 'going too far' may be huge and long-lasting, there is something even more serious at stake. Jesus tells us that our spiritual health is more important than our physical health because it has an eternal significance: 'Do not fear those who kill the body but cannot kill the soul. Rather fear him who can destroy both soul and body in hell' (Matthew 10:28). The 'killing of the soul' through sexual immorality is referred to in the passage about the adulteress in Proverbs 5:5 (NIV): 'Her feet go down to death; her steps lead straight to the grave'.

Physical intimacy before marriage takes away a God-given innocence and makes us feel guilty—this is our conscience warning us that we are over-stepping God's boundaries. Such an awareness is clear from Mary's testimony when she was encouraged by her boyfriend to go too far:

I felt guilty and ashamed after I had been physically intimate with my boyfriend, particularly with my first boyfriend. It was the first time I had crossed those boundaries and my conscience was not yet hardened. I kept thinking other people (especially my parents) would know simply by looking at me, because I felt so different. I was also worried that my boyfriend would think differently of me and that he would lose interest in me as a person.

I felt different. The truth is that I was different. I had disobeyed God and had lost my innocence because I had experienced things God had never intended me to experience at that time in my life.

Persisting in disobedience paralyses our spiritual growth and our ability to be effective for God. We are threatening the very home of the Holy Spirit when we sin sexually: 'Flee from sexual immorality. Every other sin a person commits is outside the body, but the sexually immoral person sins against his own body. Or do you not know that your body is a temple of the Holy Spirit within you, whom you have from God?' (1 Corinthians 6:18–19).

Here is how Mary described it:

My church and youth group attendance suffered. Part of this was due to the 'exclusiveness' of the relationship. I would say it is always a bad sign if you only want to spend time alone together. Relationships should always be open to the light of God's word and to the observance of godly people. I began to read my Bible less and pray less, and most of my prayers became self-centred. I seemed to spend all my time repenting and yet would find myself doing the same things I had repented of very soon after.

Relationships should always be open to the light of God's word and to the observance of godly people.

You may damage your relationship

Contrary to what many people think, exerting physical self-control helps rather than hinders a relationship. We have already seen that the emphasis in going out should not be on physical intimacy—if you are constantly wanting to go as far as you can in physical involvement, your motives and practices in the relationship are wrong. It is hard, if not impossible, to get to know someone and decide if your characters, interests and futures are compatible when you are preoccupied with physical intimacy.

> ❧
> *It is hard, if not impossible, to get to know someone and decide if your characters, interests and futures are compatible when you are preoccupied with physical intimacy.*
> ❧

Self-control allows you to enjoy the relationship free from physical distractions and a sense of guilt, and will enable you to test the relationship out effectively. It will allow you to grow individually and together without being compromised by 'sin which clings so closely' (Hebrews 12:1).

Sexual sin ...

... is sin against your own body. *1 Corinthians 6:18–19*

... dishonours God because His Spirit lives in a Christian. *1 Corinthians 6:19–20*

The consequences of sexual sin

- David's adultery with Bathsheba had spiritual, family and political consequences. *2 Samuel 12:1–15*

- It can trap you and lead to destruction. *Proverbs 5:20–23*

- It can cause spiritual and physical death. *Proverbs 6:32*

- It can cause social downfall. *Proverbs 5:3–14*

8

Thinking of the future

Look ahead and make a determined decision to keep sexual intimacy, and all that leads up to sexual intercourse, for marriage. Hear again from Jane who is now in her twenties and looks back, wishing that she had thought ahead about this important issue before the pressure of a relationship persuaded her to do something wrong:

I had a sexual relationship with a boyfriend when I was fourteen years old, at a time when I had not thought much about my own ideas on sex—whether it was right or wrong and what I really wanted in my life. I now see the huge impact that decision has had on my life. I see how important it is to make decisions about these things before getting into a relationship where the pressure to say 'yes' can be massive.

By acting in a pure way now, you will keep your marriage bed 'pure' (Hebrews 13:4), whether or not you decide to marry your current boy/girlfriend. Keeping sex for marriage is one of the best investments you can make for your future. Sexual purity will bless and protect you. Here are just some of the reasons given in this book:

1. God knows best. He made you and knows how you work. If your Designer and Creator says that marriage is the only right place for sexual activity, it is worth paying attention.

2. God says, 'Flee from sexual immorality' (1 Corinthians 6:18). The word translated 'immorality' means

all forms of sexual intimacy outside marriage.

3. A life of obedience will bring lasting fruitfulness for His kingdom (John 15:1–11).

4. You are threatening the home of the Holy Spirit when you sin sexually (1 Corinthians 6:18–19).

5. It is hard, if not impossible, to get to know someone and decide if your characters, interests and futures are compatible when you are preoccupied with physical intimacy.

6. You avoid the life-long shame and pain of extra-marital sexual experience that many have suffered.

7. You will be free of sexually transmitted infections and, if you do marry, the shame and fear of bringing these infections into your marriage.

8. You avoid getting (her) pregnant at the wrong time.

9. You avoid entering marriage with a 'past'. If you do marry, you can discover the pleasure of sexual intimacy for the first time with your husband or wife.

10. Exercising self-control now will establish trust. If you do marry, this will help to make a secure marriage.

Supremely, your obedience will glorify God (1 Corinthians 6:20). Ask God for strength to honour Him in this way.

Let us hear from Michael, who looks back over more than thirty years of married life:

The companionship which my wife and I have shared has become deeper with time. By sharing the times of great happiness, such as our wedding and later the birth of our children, as well as facing difficulties together, our relationship of love and trust has grown stronger.

Security in our marriage has been a product of being faithful, being thoughtful and being forgiving. It has been good to resolve any tensions before going to sleep, by apologising and asking forgiveness for wrongs done. The strength of our mutual love has produced a secure home for our children. The security of our family home has been shared with others as we have reached out to our neighbours, our children and our children's friends.

Imperfect as we are, we have known Christ's daily forgiveness in our lives and our marriage. The intimate bond of a sexual relationship was worth waiting for. The sacredness of this unique relationship has been part of the cement that has held our marriage together.

If we keep our best for marriage and give our best to marriage, then marriage will not disappoint us.

If we keep our best for marriage and give our best to marriage, then marriage will not disappoint us.

What to do if you have made mistakes

Reading this book may have left you with an unpleasant awareness of guilt before God. If so, you join a very large number of other Christian brothers and sisters— indeed, none of us is sexually innocent. You may even think that your sins have been too serious or too persistent for you to receive forgiveness from God. It is tempting to respond to this sense of guilt by crawling away in despair or by trying to ignore it in the hope that it will disappear. Mary experienced similar feelings after she had been physically intimate with her boyfriend. She says:

> I became convinced that God couldn't possibly still love me because I was such an awful person. It took years for me to believe that God could forgive me when I had truly repented. It also took years for me to realise that, in the midst of my sin, He loved me still. That still amazes me.

The Christian good news is the only and complete answer to this awareness of guilt. It offers the hope of forgiveness and a new start. Those who have fallen short of God's standard through sexual sin can know complete forgiveness through faith in the Lord Jesus Christ because He has already paid the full price for our sin when He died on the cross.

Remember, too, Paul's words of great assurance: 'There is therefore now no condemnation for those who are in Christ Jesus. For the law of the Spirit of life has set you free in Christ Jesus from the law of sin and death' (Romans 8:1–2). If you have been saved by the Lord Jesus, then you will not face condemnation on Judgement Day for what you have done.

And when you recognise that you have not lived up to God's standards, He requires that you do something definite in response:

- You need to say 'sorry' to God for what you have done, and ask Him to forgive you because of what Jesus has done for you on the cross.

- You need to resolve before God not to make the same mistakes again. That is what repentance means—a true turning to God away from your sin. You need to ask God to motivate you to be obedient in your actions and strengthen you to resist all future temptation.

- Remember that this resolution will mean taking practical steps to avoid all similar temptations in the future (e.g. deciding on boundaries in a relationship, learning to use a computer wisely).

- You should say sorry to those you have hurt, if this is possible.

- You should look for a (possibly older) Christian to whom you can be accountable in this area.

'If we confess our sins, he is faithful and just to forgive us our sins and cleanse us from all unrighteousness' (1 John 1:9).

Helpful Bible References

Pleasing God in our lives
- The two states of life that are pleasing to God are single and sexually inactive, or married and sexually active. *Matthew 19:3–12*

- Seek to honour God above everything. *Matthew 6:33*

Singleness ...
... is a gift from God. *1 Corinthians 7:7*

... allows you the freedom to work for the Lord without the concerns and responsibilities of marriage. *1 Corinthians 7:32–35*

Reasons for singleness

- Some people are single and sexually inactive through no choice of their own. *Matthew 19:12a*

- Some people choose to be single and sexually inactive for the kingdom of heaven. *Matthew 19:12b*

Marriage ...

... was created by God. *Genesis 2:24* and *Matthew 19:4–5*

... is a gift from God. *1 Corinthians 7:7*

God created marriage ...

... to provide companionship. *Genesis 2:18*

... to produce and nurture children. *Genesis 1:28*

The design of marriage

- It is to be lifelong. *Matthew 19:6b*

- It is to be between a man and a woman. *Matthew 19:4–5*

- It should be between only one

husband and one wife. *1 Corinthians 7:2*

- A Christian should marry a Christian. *2 Corinthians 6:14*

Additional points on marriage
- It illustrates God's love for His church. *Ephesians 5:25–32*

- It can provide protection from sexual temptation. *1 Corinthians 7:36*

- It is to be honoured by all. *Hebrews 13:4*

- It is demanding on time and energy. 1 Corinthians *7:32–35*

- It is for this world only (i.e. not in heaven). *Matthew 22:30*

Sex ...
... was created by God. *Genesis 2:24*

... is a good gift from God. *Genesis 1:31*

The purposes of sex ...
... to strengthen marriage. *Genesis 2:24*

... to produce children. *Genesis 4:1*

Sexual intimacy is only for marriage

- *Genesis 2:24*

- *Ephesians 5:3*

- *Hebrews 13:4*

- *Exodus 20:14*

Sexual sin ...

... is sin against your own body. *1 Corinthians 6:18–19*

... dishonours God because His Spirit lives in a Christian. *1 Corinthians 6:19–20*

The consequences of sexual sin

- David's adultery with Bathsheba had spiritual, family and political consequences. *2 Samuel 12:1–15*

- It can trap you and lead to destruction. *Proverbs 5:20–23*

- It can cause spiritual and physical death. *Proverbs 6:32*

- It can cause social downfall. *Proverbs 5:3–14*

Godly attitudes in going out and marriage
- Seek sexual purity. *Ephesians 5:3*

- Seek to obey God's word. *Psalm 119:9*

- Seek God's strength to be obedient. *Philippians 4:13*

- Be loving and forgiving. *Colossians 3:12–14, 1 Corinthians 13*

- Remember that obedience to God's commands brings fruitfulness and blessing. *Deuteronomy 30:15–16*

- Trust God's wisdom, not your own. *Proverbs 3:5–8*

- Trust God's good provision for His children. *Psalm 23*

How to make wise decisions
- Be prayerful. *Matthew 26:41*

- Be content in your situation. *Philippians 4:10–13*

- Take advice from the spiritually wise around you. *Proverbs 12:15* and *Proverbs 22:17*

- Avoid rash commitments. *Proverbs 20:25*

- Avoid ungodly peer pressure. *Exodus 23:2*

Endnotes

1. See Hsu, A. (1998) *The Single Issue*. IVP, for a fuller coverage of this issue.

2. See, 'Why marriage matters: Thirty conclusions from social sciences' (2012) Institute of American Values, available on-line from www.americanvalues.org

3. Bonhoeffer. D. (1997) *Letters and Papers from Prison*. New York: Touchstone, pp. 27–28.

4. For more information see James, S. (2013) *The Meaning of Marriage*. Twickenham: Family Education Trust.

5. Brandon, G. and Hayward, J. (2010) *Cohabitation in*

the 21st Century. Cambridge: The Jubilee Centre p. 2. See also Morgan, P. (2000) *Marriage-lite: The Rise of Cohabitation and its Consequences.* London: Institute for the Study of Civil Society p. 68.

6. See information from The Office of National Statistics accessible at, http://www.ons.gov.uk/ons/rel/vsob1/divorces-in-england-and-wales/2011/sty-what-percentage-of-marriages-end-in-divorce.html

7. O'Neill R. (2002) *Does Marriage Matter?* London: CIVITAS p.4 accessible at http://www.civitas.org.uk/pdf/cs31.pdf

8. Ibid, p. 5.

9. Benson, H. (May 2013) Census data analysed in *The myth of "long-term stable relationships" outside marriage.* The Marriage Foundation, accessible at www.marriagefoundation.org.uk

10. Busby, Dean M., Carroll, Jason S., Willoughby, Brian J., (December 2010) 'Compatibility or restraint? The effects of sexual timing on marriage relationships'. *Journal of Family Psychology,* Vol 24(6), pp. 766–774.

11. Morgan, P. (2000) *Marriage-lite: The Rise of Cohabitation and its Consequences.* London: Institute for the Study of Civil Society, Chapter 4.

12. Pollock, N. (1998) *The Relationships Revolution*. Leicester: IVP, p. 96.

13. For more details on this issue see Edwards, B. (1996) *Men, Women and Authority*. Day One Publications.

14. See Ash, C. (2003) *Marriage—Sex in the Service of God*. Leicester: IVP, pp. 214–216, for a detailed study on the meaning of this word.

15. Sir Paul Coleridge, senior High Court judge, quoted by Bingham, J. in 'Don't have children unless you are ready to marry, says judge', *The Daily Telegraph*, 8th December 2013, p. 1.

16. Richardson, J. (1998) *God, Sex and Marriage*. London: St Matthias Press, p. 65.

17. See, for example, an interview with Ted Bundy on www.focusonthefamily.com

18. For example, The True Freedom Trust (www.truefreedomtrust.co.uk)

19. 'Typical use' estimates include inconsistent use, incorrect use, breakage and slippage.

20. 'Workshop Summary: Scientific Evidence on Condom Effectiveness for STD Prevention', (July 20

2001) accessible at http://www.niaid.nih.gov/dmid/ stds/condomreport.pdf.

21. Savage, E. J. et al. (2012) 'Rapid increase in gonorrhoea and syphilis diagnoses in England in 2011', *Euro Surveillance*, Vol. 17(29).

22. Low, N., Geisler, W. M., Stephenson, J. M., Hook, E. W. (2013) 'Chlamydia control: A comparative review from the USA and UK', *The New Public Health and STD/HIV Prevention*, pp. 401–429.

23. McGarrigle, C. A. et al. (2006) 'Estimating adult HIV prevalence in the UK in 2003: the direct method of estimation', *Sexually Transmitted Infections*, Vol. 82 (iii), pp. 78–86.

24. Turner, C. F. et al. (2002) 'Untreated gonococcal and chlamydial infection in a probability sample of adults', *The Journal of the American Medical Association*, Vol. 287(6), pp. 726–733.

25. See Centers for Disease Control and Prevention factsheet accessible at http://www.cdc.gov/nchhstp/ newsroom/docs/STDs-Women-042011.pdf

26. Aral, S. O. and Guinan, M. E. (1984) 'Women and sexually transmitted diseases', *Sexually Transmitted Diseases*, Vol. 1, pp. 85–89.

27. Edwards, S. and Carne, C. (1998) 'Oral sex and the transmission of viral STIs', *Sexually Transmitted Infections*, Vol. 74(1), pp. 6–10. See also Edwards, S. and Carne, C. (1998) 'Oral sex and the transmission of non-viral STIs', *Sexually Transmitted Infections*, Vol. 74(2), pp. 95–100.

28. Fleming, D. T. and Wasserheit, J. N. (1999) 'From epidemiological synergy to public health policy and practice: the contribution of other sexually transmitted diseases to sexual transmission of HIV infection', *Sexually Transmitted Infections*, Vol. 75(1), pp.3–17. See also Robinson, N. J. (1997) 'Proportion of HIV infections attributable to other sexually transmitted diseases in a rural Ugandan population: simulation model estimates', *International Journal of Epidemiology*, Vol. 26(1), pp. 180–189.

29. Holmes, K. K., Levine, R. and Weaver, M. (2004) 'Effectiveness of condoms in preventing sexually transmitted infections', *Bulletin of the World Health Organisation*, Vol. 82(6), pp.454–61. See also 'Barrier Methods for Contraception and STI Prevention', (August 2012), accessible at http://www.fsrh.org/pdfs/CEUGuidanceBarrierMethodsAug12.pdf

30. Manhart, L. E. and Koutsky, L. A. (2002) 'Do condoms prevent genital HPV infection, external genital warts, or cervical neoplasia? A meta-analysis', *Sexually*

Transmitted Diseases, Vol. 29(11), pp. 725–35, accessible at: http://www.ncbi.nlm.nih.gov/pubmed/12438912

31. Hingston, R.W., Strunin, L., Berlin, B.M., Heeren, T., (1990) 'Beliefs about AIDS, use of alcohol and drugs, and unprotected sex among Massachusetts adolescents'. *American Journal of Public Health*, Vol 80(3), pp. 295–299.